Charles W. Egremont, George M.-D. Halifax

A Letter to the Right Honourable the Earls of Egremont and Halifax

His Majesty's principal secretaries of state, on the seizure of papers

Charles W. Egremont, George M.-D. Halifax

A Letter to the Right Honourable the Earls of Egremont and Halifax
His Majesty's principal secretaries of state, on the seizure of papers

ISBN/EAN: 9783337195816

Printed in Europe, USA, Canada, Australia, Japan

Cover: Foto ©Suzi / pixelio.de

More available books at **www.hansebooks.com**

A

L E T T E R

To the E A R L S of

Egremont and Halifax.

A
LETTER

TO THE

Right Honourable the Earls of

EGREMONT and HALIFAX,

His Majesty's Principal Secretaries of State,

ON THE

SEIZURE

OF

PAPERS.

LONDON:

Printed for J. WILLIAMS, near the Mitre Tavern,
Fleet-Street, 1763.

Price SIXPENCE.

A

LETTER

ON THE

SEIZURE of PAPERS.

MAY 19, 1763.

My Lords,

AMONGST the variety of polemical writings produced by a late affair, the SEIZURE OF PAPERS has not, fo far as I have obferved, been taken into confideration by any of the correfpondents of the public. Not one however of the points which have been agitated, is of

greater

greater importance, or more general concern, as a QUESTION OF LIBERTY, interesting in the highest degree to EVERY SUBJECT in the kingdom. Many other letters have submitted to the publick very important reflections on the *privilege of parliament* and *commitments*. I shall now take the liberty of offering my thoughts upon that great article of SEIZING PAPERS, which, I own, strikes me in a very strong light.

Bail will deliver every man from imprisonment before conviction, for any offence, not capital. An illegal commitment may be corrected by the summary interposition of the king's courts; and even personal restraint, at the worst, can only to any great degree affect the single person who suffers it. I have not yet heard of a *Habeas Corpus* to redeem papers from captivity. Commissions of gaol delivery do not extend to them, nor can they petition for trial, in order to force their liberty. It is not *He only*

whose

whofe papers are feized who is diftreffed
by it, but every perfon in the leaft connected with him, may by the moft acci-
dental circumftances imaginable be involved
in the confequences. Thefe go to the friend
and the friend's friend, and, in fhort, it
is impoffible to fay what may be the extent
of their influence.

I DOUBT not but there is fome legal
method of recovering papers, as well as any
other goods, which are unlawfully detained
from the right owner; but I am fure the
remedy muft, from the nature of the thing,
be very ineffectual, if it was lefs tedious and
troublefome, than I dare fay it is, as well as
all other proceedings at law. The mifchief
and damages occafioned by the feizure of
papers muft in every cafe be very great,
in many infinite, and irreparable; fuch as
no confideration, no reftitution can compen-
fate, no fatisfaction indemnify.

PAPERS relate to the affairs of bufinefs
and property; the advantages, title, and fecurity

curity of which depend upon them; but that is not all. Every man, who has papers, has his secret and confidential correspondences; his private studies, researches, and pursuits, whether of profit, entertainment, or improvement. His *papers* contain all these. The merchant has his secrets of trade; the philosopher his discoveries in science. Every accurate man has the impenetrable secret of his circumstances; the state of his affairs. Many have their WILLS, *settlements*, and dispositions of their estates, sealed up in silence, not to be broke, but with their own heart-strings. These are to be found among their *papers*. A man's riches may be there in things known to none but himself; and his poverty may from thence *only* appear, the unseasonable discovery of which may involve him in irreparable ruin. *Papers* are the depositories of our fortune; the trustees of our credit, character, and reputation; the secretaries of our pleasures. They are our closest confidents; the most intimate companions of our bosom; and, next to the

recesses

receffes of our own breafts, they are the moft hidden repofitory we can have. Our honour and fame, our eftates, our amufements, our enjoyments, our friendfhips, *are*, and even our vices *may be*, there : things that men truft none with, but themfelves ; things upon which the peace and quiet of families, the love and union of relations, the prefervation and value of friends, depend. Secrets that may coft a man his life ; fecrets (of which there are many) that tho' they can neither affect life nor liberty, yet fome men would rather die than have difcovered ; the revealing of which may render life infupportable, may diffolve every tie of nature, loofen every bond of fociety, and put an utter end to the comfort of exiftence.

I t is for thefe reafons, that wife men not only keep their papers with the greateft care, but at convenient feafons purge their repofitories, and deftroy thofe that ought not to be preferved, after the immediate purpofes of them are anfwered. They have above all, a fpecial care into whofe hands their secret papers shall come, after they are dead ; a precaution that every man owes not only to himself, but to his family and friends, perhaps to his country.

BUT what need is there to enlarge upon such a topick? Every man's own mind will represent the thing to him in a stronger light, than any language can convey. Let any person, the most private and the least employed, or concerned, in business, study, or correspondence, pause only a moment, and consider if he would choose to have his closet ransacked, his most private repositories rifled, his papers carried he knows not where, and exposed to he knows not whom. Let him likewise reflect, that in this matter every man is dependent upon another, in a singular, but unavoidable manner, to an unspeakable, but inextricable degree; and that every person may in a great measure, or to an equal effect, suffer the same inconveniencies from the misfortunes happening to his friend, as if it had befallen himself:

So

fo that in proportion to the extent of a man's connections, and correspondence, is he expofed to this hardfhip, and to all the mifchievous confequences of it.

THE moft fuperficial thought upon thefe things will fuperfede the ufe of any argument to convince mankind of the important mifchiefs attendant on a SEIZURE OF PAPERS, or to fatisfy them, that perfonal liberty itfelf is not an object of greater concern than the fecurity of repofitories is to moft men.

Is it not then abundantly provided for? It is to be hoped, that it *is* by the law of the land; but it would feem the prefent practice of the fecretaries of ftate's office pays no regard at all to it; if what has been publifhed to all the world be true. It has not been contradicted; on the contrary, it is acknowledged.

The parliament, to make private correfpondence facred, has enacted that a fingle letter fhall not under the higheft penalties be opened at the Poft-office, with-

out

out an exprefs warrant in writing from a fecretary of ftate, in whom that particular
power is lodged, as one of the firft minifters
of government. What fhall we fay then,
when we hear that a perfon (it is of very
little confequence who, but it does not lef-
fen the importance of the confideration, that
he is a MEMBER OF PARLIAMENT) has
had ALL HIS PAPERS SEIZED, without in-
formation upon OATH, by virtue of a VER-
BAL ORDER of a fecretary of ftate, whofe
powers as a magiftrate (in which character
only he acts in this inftance) are no higher,
it feems, than thofe of a juftice of peace :
an ORDER which the fecretary of ftate com-
manded to be carried into execution at
MIDNIGHT, though the meffenger had
either too much humanity or too little confidence in his authority, to obey that part
of the order; or perhaps had a greater value
for his life, than to expofe it in fo mad an
exploit, as a midnight entry into a man's
houfe without fo much as the pretence of a
warrant *naming the owner*.

THE

THE PAPERS have been carried to the
fecretary of ftate's office; and there (as
your own letters intimate) they have been
thoroughly examined. The news papers have already publifhed fome of the
privacies contained in them. Is this LAW?
Is it LIBERTY? Is it GOVERNMENT? Or
is it TYRANNY and OPPRESSION? If it is
LAW, where is LIBERTY? If it is NOT
LAW, where is the VOICE of LIBERTY?

BUT can there be SUCH LAW, in
this FREE COUNTRY? One cannot furely
read it in the CONSTITUTION; and if
it is in the ftatute book, or in the record
of any court in the kingdom, it ought
not to remain a moment longer capable
of being quoted to difgrace the BEST
form of GOVERNMENT, and difquiet the
FREEST PEOPLE. No Englifhman till
he fees it read or is informed of it, can
believe that there is fuch a law in this LAND
OF LIBERTY. SLAVERY itfelf could
hardly endure it. It muft be the HEAVI-
 EST

ᴇsᴛ Bᴏɴᴅᴀɢᴇ, even where there is ɴᴏ Fʀᴇᴇᴅᴏᴍ.

To explain the mifchievous nature and oppreffive tendency of fuch a law, if there were any fuch, is paft the power of words. To exaggerate the enormity of fuch proceedings, would be to infult the loweft underftanding in this country, where the Gᴇɴɪᴜs ᴏꜰ Lɪʙᴇʀᴛʏ reigns. Such acts are little fhort of Sᴀᴄʀɪʟᴇɢᴇ.

Wᴇ are however told by one Perfon in your office that every ftep was taken by the *attorney* and *folicitor general*'s advice. Tʜᴀᴛ cannot be; for the moft ignorant conftable in Weftminfter could have inftructed your lordfhips that a Vᴇʀʙᴀʟ Oʀᴅᴇʀ was a warrant for ɴᴏᴛʜɪɴɢ ; and it is inconceiveable how you yourfelves could have thought otherwife. Another champion of power, who calls himfelf a *moderate whig,* vindicates the whole proceeding by faying with a perfpecuity peculiar to his own ftile, " The length
of

" of time and feveral precedents *may not*
" conftitute an act ftrictly legal, which *may*
" *not* be literally fo *(thefe are his own*
" *unintelligible words)* yet it will acquit
" thofe who act conformable to precedents
" before uncontroverted, and believed
" to be legal, from any defign of acting
" illegally, in the opinion of every honeft
" man."

How there can be a precedent, unlefs
in unauthentick memory, for a *verbal or-der*, is not fo eafy to be underftood. This
inftance will make none; for no body
doubts of the illegality of it. The precedents of the fecretary of ftate's office however, if there was a cart load of them, are
of no authority. If they have never been
controverted, then it only appears that they
have not *yet* been judicially difputed. Hi-
therto, it is to be feared, it has been too
much *fragili quærens illidere dentem*, now it
may be found to be *offendet folido*. The regifter
of Sir John Fielding's warrants deferves to
carry more weight with it than the book of
the

the fecretary of ftate's office. If *that* was fent to your office for a copy book, your lord-fhips, or at leaft your fucceffors, would not hereafter caufe any perfon to be apprehended by a WARRANT that NAMES NO BODY; which of itfelf is an offence for which a chief juftice in a former reign has been impeached.

THIS ridiculous talk of precedents is fhocking to the firft idea of a FREE Government. They ought not to be once mentioned. They muft at the name of LIBERTY fhrink back into the gloomy caverns of tyranny, where fuch vulcanian thunder bolts only could be forged; as fpectres retreat to their difmal fhades at the words of a true exorcifm.

THERE is indeed hardly any thing fo wicked, or unconftitutional, but a precedent may be found for it, if the records of the ftar chamber, or the memorials of tyranny, are referted to as authorities. The great ALGERNON SYDNEY, whofe valuable blood prepared the foil for receiving
the

the feeds of the GLORIOUS REVOLUTION, was executed for high treafon ; and the overt act for which he died on a profane fcaffold, was that precious MANUSCRIPT found in his clofet, which never had been publifhed, and was not completed ; the hand-writing of which was not proved, a fiftieth part of it not produced, nor even the tenth part of *that* allowed to be read at the trial.

But *in whofe reign* was this cruel tragedy acted? In the BLOODY reign of *a Stuart*, Charles the Second, an unhappy prince, who facrificed the lives of the very people who called him from exile, to the fury of his defpotifm, and who fold the honour of his crown for a penfion to fupport his infamous pleafures.—Who condemned the noble MARTYR of liberty? That arch traitor of his country, the moft infamous inftrument of regal tyranny, and a very butcher of his own fpecies, Lord Chief Juftice JEFFRIES of ROTTEN MEMORY.

LOOK to the reigns of a glorious WILLIAM, who nobly refcued and happily re-

D   ftored,

ſtored, and of the ILLUSTRIOUS GEORGES, who to their immortal honour, have built up, this INVALUABLE CONSTITUTI-ON; PRINCES who have read the value of ENGLISH LIBERTY in the luſtre of the crown which IT placed upon their heads; PRINCES who have eſtabliſhed the ſecurity of the PROTESTANT SUCCESSION in their own auguſt family upon the ſame baſis with the ENVIED FREEDOM of THESE NA-TIONS; the pillars of which are not to be ſhaken.

FROM *theſe reigns* can there be produced a precedent of *legal authority* for *ſuch* a SEIZURE OF PAPERS as has happened late-ly? Do their days ſo much as furniſh an *allowed* example of the fact to the ſame ex-tent? It may be doubted if in the very worſt of times, when arbitrary principles were riſing to the top of the precipice, from which at laſt tyranny fell head-long with its own weight, ſuch things were *avowedly* practiſed under the *ſhew* of authority; what-ever *meer power*, or rather *force*, as irregular in its acts, as unconſtitutional in its foun-dation, might perhaps do. BUT

BUT what was the pretence of this late violation of rights fo facred in their nature, this invafion of property, in a critical point, which comprehends every valuable interest a man can have? A perfon is fufpected of being the author of a printed paper, which, in the judgment of the fecretaries of ftate, was a feditious libel, and the proof of the fact is to be fifted out of his *own* papers: for your lordfhips have faid in your letter, which is publifhed, that fuch of the papers feized, as tend to make out the guilt of the owner are to be kept, and ufed for that purpofe.

THE reafon is moft inadequate, and muft appear fo to every man, who is not beat out of his fenfes by the jargon of lawyers, or confounded in his own ideas with the quibbles of legal nonfenfe.

IF there is a circumftance that can aggravate the injury, which is in itfelf too great almoft to be conceived, it is this ufe that is to be made of the papers; and nothing

can

cán so much add to the ALARM which the
practice of SEIZING OF PAPERS muft give
to every man.

WHEN a perfon is brought upon his trial
for any offence, he is not bound, nor will
any court fuffer him to give evidence againft
himfelf; but by this method, if allowed,
though a man's tongue is not permitted to
bear teftimony againft him, his thoughts are
to rife in judgment, and to be produced as
witneffes to prove the charge. A man's
WRITINGS lying in his clofet, NOT PUB-
LISHED, are no more than his thoughts,
hardly brought forth even in his own ac-
count, and, to all the reft of the world, the
fame as if they yet remained in embrio in
his breaft. When ALL a man's PA-
PERS are feized, he is at the mercy of
his profecutors. Some may be ufed to prove
a charge, when others, which are *fuppref-
fed*, would clearly exculpate him of guilt. It
was thus in the infamous proceedings which
robbed that hero of patriotifm, the great
SYDNEY, of his life. *Scraps* of an *unfinifhed
manufcript*

manuscript were the evidences upon which he was condemned, when the rest of that very writing was not produced.

THE rack itself is hardly a more inhuman mode of accusation, or tyrannical method of proof. Both are equally against the first laws of nature; and nothing can be more unlike the benign spirit of our happy constitution.

IN cases of treason papers are seized, tho' even *then* it is always done with much circumspection, and under many restrictions as to the use to be made of them; but *that* proceeds upon a quite different principle, a principle of sense and reason.

TREASON, in the general nature of it, must be the crime of *many*. It implies plots and conspiracies, which are carrying on by correspondence, and are to be discovered by *papers*. The safety of the state, which is superior to every other consideration, makes it necessary, to use all possible means

means to unmaſk the machinations of *treaſon*, that the dreadful effects may be pre-
vented. *Papers* therefore may be. ſeized,
and letters intercepted, as arms, ammunition,
and other warlike ſtores may be ſecured, that
the ſinews of rebellion may be cut. This
is the ſole reaſon, and end of ſeizing
papers, in a *treaſonable* caſe, although they
may afterwards be uſed as proofs of ſuch
overt acts of *treaſon* as they are connected
with, or bear relation to, ſo as to make
them be conſidered as a part of the proſecu-
tion of the ſame *treaſonable* purpoſes; yet
ſurely it cannot be law even in caſes of *treaſon*, nor (we hope) ever was law, with any
but ſuch a judge as Lord Chief Juſtice *Jeffries*, that *papers* found in a man's cloſet,
not publiſhed, and unconnected with any
thing but themſelves, can conſtitute a crime,
or be brought as a proof of guilt.

WHAT *does* however hold in *treaſon*,
will not take place in other caſes. There
is a certain neceſſary rigour and ſeverity
in the laws of *treaſon*, which would
be cruelty, if extended to other crimes.
Many

Many things are allowed in the cafe of treafon, that, if applied to other matters, would
be more mifchievous in their confequences
than the things they were intended to prevent.

IT is *treafon* to compafs or imagine (as it
is called) or, in plain Englifh, to contrive or
intend the death of the king, if it can be
proved by any overt act; and it could be
no more than *treafon* actually to put the fo-
vereign to death. It is not however mur-
der, *in foro humano*, to intend, or even to attempt to kill another man. There is therefore no example to be drawn from what *is*
or *may be* done in cafes of *treafon*, to any
other cafe ; and none can be more unfimilar
to it than that of libels.

PUBLICATION is effential to a libel, and
the criminality is intrinfick in itfelf. The
offence, and the effects of it, both ftand upon
the libel *alone*, unconnected with any other
thing whatfoever. There is not therefore the
leaft colour of danger, or neceffity, to plead

for breaking through any right, or any privilege of the fubject, for the fake of difcovery or prevention, in fuch a cafe; much lefs to trample upon thofe rights that are the moft facred and inviolable, and the confequences of injuring them pernicious beyond expreffion. The evil is great; the mifchief apparent. The utility and good is nothing, or fo inconfiderable, as to be no object at all.

To the mercy of *any* government even convicts may have fome claim; the benignity of *ours*, guilt itfelf cannot forfeit. Its fuavity, and mildnefs, in profecutions and trials, can be denied, or interrupted to none. Sufpicion, or accufation, do not annul the rights of innocence; nor rob the fubject, either of the protection, or *favour* of the laws. The *lenity* of juftice is, in England, its *dignity*. Fair trials, and *gentle* profecutions, are the peculiar glory of this country; and no man fhould be deprived of any benefit, or advantage, his own filence, or the fecrecy of papers *not publifhed*, can afford to protect him againft conviction. As he can

keep

keep his mouth fhut, fo his privacies ought
to be facred, and his repofitories fecure.

BUT if the partitions of a man's
clofet, (which is but another bofom,) are to
be wantonly broke down, on every flight
pretence, or trivial occafion, and what lies
there locked up in fecrecy, things that the
world never faw, and no man has a right
to look upon, are to be expofed at the hu-
mour or malice of every, perhaps trading,
juftice of peace, (for fo far it goes) let the
moft partial determine what muft be the
confequences. There is an END OF LIBER-
TY, an end of confidence amongft mankind.
A fevere reftraint is laid upon friendfhip and
correfpondence, and even upon the freedom
of thought. In fhort, a FATAL BLOW is
given to the moft precious and valuable rights
of mankind; to the faireft privileges of fociety.
The thing is big with mifchiefs innumerable,
and inconceivable; the leaft of them not to
be laid in the balance with all the danger
of any *libel* the moft feditious that can be
publifhed, or with any thing lefs than *high*

E   *treafon*

treafon itfelf, which does, and juftly ought
to overcome all rights whatfoever of any
individual, be the confequences what they
may. If care is taken in that cafe, that no
harm be done which can poffibly be avoid-
ed, nor any unneceffary hardfhips inflicted,
it is all that can be expected, and as much
as ought to be required.

PRECEDENTS of feizing the *papers* of
printers, and publifhers, are comparatively
fcarce worthy having any notice taken of
them in a juft and accurate confideration of
this fubject. The papers and repofitories of
every private perfon ftand upon a very different
foot. If amongft *thefe* any diftinction can be
made, it is due to the cafe of MEMBERS OF
PARLIAMENT, for the fake of their TRUST,
and of the intereft their conftituents have in
their freedom, fecurity, and independency.
On thefe all our valuable rights depend;
and they cannot be expofed to a greater or
more dangerous INFRINGEMENT than an
undue SEIZURE OF PAPERS. It has always, for this reafon, been the GREAT
OBJECT

OBJECT of the HOUSE OF COMMONS, to protect the Members of Parliament from such illegal invasions.

THE publick may, perhaps, be thought to have some more power over those, who are a sort of servants of the publick than over *private* persons ; and professed publishers (in the case of publications) are a sort of publick persons. Their shops and offices, therefore, are in some sense, and to a limited degree, the houses of the publick.

THESE kind of people, however, all the world knows, are soon frightened, and intimidation speedily checks them. Ministers know it ; and therefore they use it without scruple, and without mercy, when *they* think fit. How far that is consistent with the LIBERTY OF THE PRESS, or for the advantage of the public, is another question.

THE authority of a secretary of state, even a hint from the office, and much more

E 2   appre-

apprehenfions, examinations, and menaces, will foon conquer thefe poor men's ideas of liberty, and make them fond to redeem themfelves. They are very ready to purchafe exemption from a hard, expenfive, and dangerous profecution, directed by power and carried on from the public purfe, at the expence of fubmitting to acts illegal, and oppreffive, for which a court of law, and an Englifh jury would give ample redrefs and fatisfaction. No ftrefs whatever can therefore be laid on fuch inftances, if any can be cited ; but, at any rate, precedents of *fact* are not at all, or in any cafe, to be regarded. LEGAL PRECEDENTS are thofe whofe authority ftands upon trial, and judicial decifions of courts of law, in TIMES OF LIBERTY, and JUSTICE.

IF there have been any examples of undue *feizure of papers*, fo far from being precedents to *juftify*, or even to *excufe* the practice, they afford the ftrongeft reafon in the world for giving a timely and effectual check to it; that it may no longer

continue

continue to be the *grief* and *burthen* of the subject.

PRECEDENTS which have the *shew* of authority, from the sanction of courts, though of arbitrary and unjust judges, in times too of tyranny and oppression, can only be mentioned to be scorned, and inveigh'd against, in days of LIBERTY and JUSTICE; or to be set up as beacons to warn against the shipwrecks, which the rocks and quick-sands of arbitrary power have occasioned, in former ages.

BUT in the halcyon days of LIBERTY, when JUSTICE is administred with PURITY, care will be had to avoid precedents of *seeming* authority, to give to proceedings that are *arbitrary*, and oppressive, the appearance of being *legal*. It is the more necessary to do it, because precedents of such times will have weight from the character of the times. Bad and illegal precedents of *fact* cannot be too soon, nor too severely corrected ; not only for the

honour

honour of the government, and the prefent
fecurity of the fubject, but that they may
not remain to be quoted in fucceeding, and in
worfe times, if fuch fhall ever be the curfe
of this country, except as authorities *againft*
any attempt to imitate the practices for-
merly condemned, and effectually to prevent
their being renewed or repeated.

EVERY TRUE FRIEND OF LIBERTY
therefore will anxioufly defire to fee this
queftion have a fair trial , that he may know
exactly how the law ftands, and be fully ap-
prized of his danger ; fo that all may provide
againft it the beft they can. If on every
pretence or fufpicion of a libel, or of what
not only a fecretary of ftate, but the
loweft magiftrate of the peace, may pleafe
to deem one, in which POLITICKS, PAR-
TY, PREJUDICE, and RESENTMENT, will
always have a great influence, OUR HOUSES,
and our FRIENDS HOUSES, are to be OPEN
at all hours and under all circumftances
to every prowling officer of the crown,
actuated by curiofity, intereft, defign, or re-
venge,

venge, he will be the wifeft man that cor-
refponds the leaft with others, and the moft
prudent who writes very little, and keeps
as few papers as he can by him. None but
a fool in this cafe will have any fecrets at all
in his poffeffion.

THAT no fuch BADGE OF SLAVERY
does *yet* exift in this country, is ftill believed.
That it never may exift will naturally be the
wifh of every ENGLISHMAN. The expec-
tations of LIBERTY are, that if the late
moft extraordinary, and, as it is thought,
unprecedented and illegal *feizure of papers*,
produces a legal trial, it will be found to
have been manifeftly AGAINST LAW; and
that all the fubjects of this kingdom will
have the fatisfaction to be affured by a judicial determination, that as their HOUSES
are their SANCTUARIES, their CLOSETS
are the SANCTUM SANCTORUM of that
Sanctuary.

I am,

Your Lordfhips, &c.